Spring has Sprung

Color By Numbers Coloring Book for Adults

ZenMaster Coloring Books

Copyright © 2018 by ZenMaster
All rights reserved. No part of this publication may be reproduced, distributed, or transmitted in any form or by any means, including photocopying, recording, or other electronic or mechanical methods, without the prior written permission of the publisher.

COLOR TEST PAGE

COLOR TEST PAGE

1. Ivory
2. Cadmium Yellow
3. Primrose Yellow
4. Cadmium Orange
5. Orange Glaze
6. Flame
7. Pink Yarrow
8. Pink Carmine
9. Fuchsia
10. Deep Red
11. Magenta
12. Crimson
13. Violet
14. Blue Violet
15. Sky Blue
16. Ultramarine
17. Cobalt Blue
18. Prussian Blue
19. Turquoise
20. Cobalt Green
21. Light Green
22. Leaf Green
23. May Green
24. Burnt Ochre
25. Bistre
26. Walnut Brown
27. Warm Grey
28. Dark Sepia

1. Ivory
2. Cadmium Yellow
3. Primrose Yellow
4. Cadmium Orange
5. Orange Glaze
6. Flame
7. Pink Yarrow
8. Pink Carmine
9. Fuchsia
10. Deep Red
11. Magenta
12. Crimson
13. Violet
14. Blue Violet
15. Sky Blue
16. Ultramarine
17. Cobalt Blue
18. Prussian Blue
19. Turquoise
20. Cobalt Green
21. Light Green
22. Leaf Green
23. May Green
24. Burnt Ochre
25. Bistre
26. Walnut Brown
27. Warm Grey
28. Dark Sepia

1. Ivory
2. Cadmium Yellow
3. Primrose Yellow
4. Cadmium Orange
5. Orange Glaze
6. Flame
7. Pink Yarrow
8. Pink Carmine
9. Fuchsia
10. Deep Red
11. Magenta
12. Crimson
13. Violet
14. Blue Violet
15. Sky Blue
16. Ultramarine
17. Cobalt Blue
18. Prussian Blue
19. Turquoise
20. Cobalt Green
21. Light Green
22. Leaf Green
23. May Green
24. Burnt Ochre
25. Bistre
26. Walnut Brown
27. Warm Grey
28. Dark Sepia

1. Ivory
2. Cadmium Yellow
3. Primrose Yellow
4. Cadmium Orange
5. Orange Glaze
6. Flame
7. Pink Yarrow
8. Pink Carmine
9. Fuchsia
10. Deep Red
11. Magenta
12. Crimson
13. Violet
14. Blue Violet
15. Sky Blue
16. Ultramarine
17. Cobalt Blue
18. Prussian Blue
19. Turquoise
20. Cobalt Green
21. Light Green
22. Leaf Green
23. May Green
24. Burnt Ochre
25. Bistre
26. Walnut Brown
27. Warm Grey
28. Dark Sepia

1. Ivory
2. Cadmium Yellow
3. Primrose Yellow
4. Cadmium Orange
5. Orange Glaze
6. Flame
7. Pink Yarrow
8. Pink Carmine
9. Fuchsia
10. Deep Red
11. Magenta
12. Crimson
13. Violet
14. Blue Violet
15. Sky Blue
16. Ultramarine
17. Cobalt Blue
18. Prussian Blue
19. Turquoise
20. Cobalt Green
21. Light Green
22. Leaf Green
23. May Green
24. Burnt Ochre
25. Bistre
26. Walnut Brown
27. Warm Grey
28. Dark Sepia

1. Ivory
2. Cadmium Yellow
3. Primrose Yellow
4. Cadmium Orange
5. Orange Glaze
6. Flame
7. Pink Yarrow
8. Pink Carmine
9. Fuchsia
10. Deep Red
11. Magenta
12. Crimson
13. Violet
14. Blue Violet
15. Sky Blue
16. Ultramarine
17. Cobalt Blue
18. Prussian Blue
19. Turquoise
20. Cobalt Green
21. Light Green
22. Leaf Green
23. May Green
24. Burnt Ochre
25. Bistre
26. Walnut Brown
27. Warm Grey
28. Dark Sepia

1. Ivory
2. Cadmium Yellow
3. Primrose Yellow
4. Cadmium Orange
5. Orange Glaze
6. Flame
7. Pink Yarrow
8. Pink Carmine
9. Fuchsia
10. Deep Red
11. Magenta
12. Crimson
13. Violet
14. Blue Violet
15. Sky Blue
16. Ultramarine
17. Cobalt Blue
18. Prussian Blue
19. Turquoise
20. Cobalt Green
21. Light Green
22. Leaf Green
23. May Green
24. Burnt Ochre
25. Bistre
26. Walnut Brown
27. Warm Grey
28. Dark Sepia

1. Ivory
2. Cadmium Yellow
3. Primrose Yellow
4. Cadmium Orange
5. Orange Glaze
6. Flame
7. Pink Yarrow
8. Pink Carmine
9. Fuchsia
10. Deep Red
11. Magenta
12. Crimson
13. Violet
14. Blue Violet
15. Sky Blue
16. Ultramarine
17. Cobalt Blue
18. Prussian Blue
19. Turquoise
20. Cobalt Green
21. Light Green
22. Leaf Green
23. May Green
24. Burnt Ochre
25. Bistre
26. Walnut Brown
27. Warm Grey
28. Dark Sepia

1. Ivory
2. Cadmium Yellow
3. Primrose Yellow
4. Cadmium Orange
5. Orange Glaze
6. Flame
7. Pink Yarrow
8. Pink Carmine
9. Fuchsia
10. Deep Red
11. Magenta
12. Crimson
13. Violet
14. Blue Violet
15. Sky Blue
16. Ultramarine
17. Cobalt Blue
18. Prussian Blue
19. Turquoise
20. Cobalt Green
21. Light Green
22. Leaf Green
23. May Green
24. Burnt Ochre
25. Bistre
26. Walnut Brown
27. Warm Grey
28. Dark Sepia

1. Ivory
2. Cadmium Yellow
3. Primrose Yellow
4. Cadmium Orange
5. Orange Glaze
6. Flame
7. Pink Yarrow
8. Pink Carmine
9. Fuchsia
10. Deep Red
11. Magenta
12. Crimson
13. Violet
14. Blue Violet
15. Sky Blue
16. Ultramarine
17. Cobalt Blue
18. Prussian Blue
19. Turquoise
20. Cobalt Green
21. Light Green
22. Leaf Green
23. May Green
24. Burnt Ochre
25. Bistre
26. Walnut Brown
27. Warm Grey
28. Dark Sepia

1. Ivory
2. Cadmium Yellow
3. Primrose Yellow
4. Cadmium Orange
5. Orange Glaze
6. Flame
7. Pink Yarrow
8. Pink Carmine
9. Fuchsia
10. Deep Red
11. Magenta
12. Crimson
13. Violet
14. Blue Violet
15. Sky Blue
16. Ultramarine
17. Cobalt Blue
18. Prussian Blue
19. Turquoise
20. Cobalt Green
21. Light Green
22. Leaf Green
23. May Green
24. Burnt Ochre
25. Bistre
26. Walnut Brown
27. Warm Grey
28. Dark Sepia

1. Ivory
2. Cadmium Yellow
3. Primrose Yellow
4. Cadmium Orange
5. Orange Glaze
6. Flame
7. Pink Yarrow
8. Pink Carmine
9. Fuchsia
10. Deep Red
11. Magenta
12. Crimson
13. Violet
14. Blue Violet
15. Sky Blue
16. Ultramarine
17. Cobalt Blue
18. Prussian Blue
19. Turquoise
20. Cobalt Green
21. Light Green
22. Leaf Green
23. May Green
24. Burnt Ochre
25. Bistre
26. Walnut Brown
27. Warm Grey
28. Dark Sepia

1. Ivory
2. Cadmium Yellow
3. Primrose Yellow
4. Cadmium Orange
5. Orange Glaze
6. Flame
7. Pink Yarrow
8. Pink Carmine
9. Fuchsia
10. Deep Red
11. Magenta
12. Crimson
13. Violet
14. Blue Violet
15. Sky Blue
16. Ultramarine
17. Cobalt Blue
18. Prussian Blue
19. Turquoise
20. Cobalt Green
21. Light Green
22. Leaf Green
23. May Green
24. Burnt Ochre
25. Bistre
26. Walnut Brown
27. Warm Grey
28. Dark Sepia

1. Ivory
2. Cadmium Yellow
3. Primrose Yellow
4. Cadmium Orange
5. Orange Glaze
6. Flame
7. Pink Yarrow
8. Pink Carmine
9. Fuchsia
10. Deep Red
11. Magenta
12. Crimson
13. Violet
14. Blue Violet
15. Sky Blue
16. Ultramarine
17. Cobalt Blue
18. Prussian Blue
19. Turquoise
20. Cobalt Green
21. Light Green
22. Leaf Green
23. May Green
24. Burnt Ochre
25. Bistre
26. Walnut Brown
27. Warm Grey
28. Dark Sepia

1. Ivory
2. Cadmium Yellow
3. Primrose Yellow
4. Cadmium Orange
5. Orange Glaze
6. Flame
7. Pink Yarrow
8. Pink Carmine
9. Fuchsia
10. Deep Red
11. Magenta
12. Crimson
13. Violet
14. Blue Violet
15. Sky Blue
16. Ultramarine
17. Cobalt Blue
18. Prussian Blue
19. Turquoise
20. Cobalt Green
21. Light Green
22. Leaf Green
23. May Green
24. Burnt Ochre
25. Bistre
26. Walnut Brown
27. Warm Grey
28. Dark Sepia

1. Ivory
2. Cadmium Yellow
3. Primrose Yellow
4. Cadmium Orange
5. Orange Glaze
6. Flame
7. Pink Yarrow
8. Pink Carmine
9. Fuchsia
10. Deep Red
11. Magenta
12. Crimson
13. Violet
14. Blue Violet
15. Sky Blue
16. Ultramarine
17. Cobalt Blue
18. Prussian Blue
19. Turquoise
20. Cobalt Green
21. Light Green
22. Leaf Green
23. May Green
24. Burnt Ochre
25. Bistre
26. Walnut Brown
27. Warm Grey
28. Dark Sepia

1. Ivory
2. Cadmium Yellow
3. Primrose Yellow
4. Cadmium Orange
5. Orange Glaze
6. Flame
7. Pink Yarrow
8. Pink Carmine
9. Fuchsia
10. Deep Red
11. Magenta
12. Crimson
13. Violet
14. Blue Violet
15. Sky Blue
16. Ultramarine
17. Cobalt Blue
18. Prussian Blue
19. Turquoise
20. Cobalt Green
21. Light Green
22. Leaf Green
23. May Green
24. Burnt Ochre
25. Bistre
26. Walnut Brown
27. Warm Grey
28. Dark Sepia

1. Ivory
2. Cadmium Yellow
3. Primrose Yellow
4. Cadmium Orange
5. Orange Glaze
6. Flame
7. Pink Yarrow
8. Pink Carmine
9. Fuchsia
10. Deep Red
11. Magenta
12. Crimson
13. Violet
14. Blue Violet
15. Sky Blue
16. Ultramarine
17. Cobalt Blue
18. Prussian Blue
19. Turquoise
20. Cobalt Green
21. Light Green
22. Leaf Green
23. May Green
24. Burnt Ochre
25. Bistre
26. Walnut Brown
27. Warm Grey
28. Dark Sepia

1. Ivory
2. Cadmium Yellow
3. Primrose Yellow
4. Cadmium Orange
5. Orange Glaze
6. Flame
7. Pink Yarrow
8. Pink Carmine
9. Fuchsia
10. Deep Red
11. Magenta
12. Crimson
13. Violet
14. Blue Violet
15. Sky Blue
16. Ultramarine
17. Cobalt Blue
18. Prussian Blue
19. Turquoise
20. Cobalt Green
21. Light Green
22. Leaf Green
23. May Green
24. Burnt Ochre
25. Bistre
26. Walnut Brown
27. Warm Grey
28. Dark Sepia

1. Ivory
2. Cadmium Yellow
3. Primrose Yellow
4. Cadmium Orange
5. Orange Glaze
6. Flame
7. Pink Yarrow
8. Pink Carmine
9. Fuchsia
10. Deep Red
11. Magenta
12. Crimson
13. Violet
14. Blue Violet
15. Sky Blue
16. Ultramarine
17. Cobalt Blue
18. Prussian Blue
19. Turquoise
20. Cobalt Green
21. Light Green
22. Leaf Green
23. May Green
24. Burnt Ochre
25. Bistre
26. Walnut Brown
27. Warm Grey
28. Dark Sepia

Thank you for supporting
ZenMaster Coloring Books!

I aim to make sure my customers have the most enjoyable and relaxing coloring experience possible and I would love to hear your feedback!

Please leave a review on Amazon and follow me on facebook for updates and free coloring pages!

https://www.facebook.com/zenmastercoloringbooks/

check out more of my books at:

amazon.com/author/zenmastercoloringbooks

Free Bonus Page!
from:

large print simple and easy
Horses
coloring book for adults
https://amzn.com/977777775

Also available in color by numbers!!
https://amzn.com/1977877176

Free Bonus Page!
from:

Large Pring Simple and Easy
Mandalas
Coloring Book For Adults

https://amzn.com/198151290X

Also available in color by numbers!!
https://amzn.com/198207616X

Made in the USA
Columbia, SC
27 February 2018